Ladies In Waiting

A Pictorial Review of Davis Monthan AFB

by Scott Wonderly & Richard Dunham

squadron/signal publications

Operation DESERT STORM marked the end of the A-7 Corsair IIs operational career with the Navy. With the end of the war, these early A-7As will soon be joined by A-7Es as the last squadrons are decomissioned. (Wonderly)

If you have any photographs of the aircraft, armor, soldiers or ships of any nation, particularly wartime snapshots, why not share them with us and help make Squadron/Signal's books all the more interesting and complete in the future. Any photograph sent to us will be copied and the original returned. The donor will be fully credited for any photos used. Please send them to:

Squadron/Signal Publications, Inc.
1115 Crowley Drive.
Carrollton, TX 75011-5010.

Dedication

Dedicated to our ladies, Gigi and Barbara, who waited several years for this fantasy to end.

Photo Credits

USAF	U.S. Navy
Smithsonian	K. Kula
J. Puzzullo	R. Weidner
J. Campbell	COL McKean (USAF)
J. Fugere	AMARC

Special Thanks

A special thank you to all of the personnel at Davis-Monthan AFB who helped us on this project, especially those in public affairs. Also to those who get up early on that one special Saturday each month and donate their time to escort airplane crazy types like us on the AMARC photographic tour.

Authors' Note

Historically ships have normally been referred to in the feminine gender and this trend has continued with aircraft right into the age of airplanes. This work is a review of the "Ladies" in storage at the Aerospace Maintenance and Regeneration Center (AMARC), Davis-Monthan AFB, as they await their next "assignment." We would like to state that AMARC is not a boneyard as some have suggested. It is a very viable activity that manages the Defense Department assets amounting to the third largest air force in the world. As such, AMARC is a phenomenal place to visit.

(Overleaf)
This B-52 Stratofortress is one of the more colorful aircraft in storage at Davis-Monthan. The aircraft was used for the CCV test program and was outfitted with movable conard control surfaces on the nose. (Wonderly)

Introduction

Davis-Monthan Air Force Base is located in a valley surrounded by five different mountain ranges. The base is home to approximately 6,000 military personnel assigned to the 868th Tactical Missile Training Group, the 602nd Tactical Air Control Wing, the 355th Tactical Training Wing, the 836th Combat Support Group, and the 71st Special Operations Squadron. Davis-Monthan, however, is far better known as the home of AMARC.

The Aerospace Maintenance and Regeneration Center (AMARC) is also very mistakenly known as the "boneyard." This title originated from the early days when no longer needed aircraft were scrapped for their aluminum. Today, more than ever, that title is misleading and false; AMARC is anything but a final resting place for old aircraft waiting to be scrapped.

1919 saw Tucson become a leader in the aviation field when the city established its first municipal airport. The airport was moved during 1921 to the present site of the air base and in 1927, Charles Lindbergh dedicated the site now known as Davis-Monthan Field.

The new airport was named for two local residents, LT Samuel H. Davis and LT Oscar Monthan. Both men had served during the First World War and both had died in military aircraft accidents. Davis died in a crash at Carlstrom Field, Florida, during 1921, while Monthan died in 1924 in a crash at Honolulu, Hawaii.

Davis-Monthan, or D-M as it is more commonly known, remained a municipal airport until 4 February 1941, when it was activated as a military training base with the mission of training bombardment aircrews for the B-18 Bolo, the B-24 Liberator and the

B-29 Superfortress. During this period, from 1941 to 1942, the name was changed to Tucson Air Base. Then in 1942, the base was rededicated as Davis-Monthan Field and in 1948 the base was officially designated Davis-Monthan Air Force Base.

When the Second World War ended, D-M training operations came to a standstill. Logistically all that remained active was a storage area for B-29s and C-47s. This area had been created by the San Antonio Air Technical Service Command immediately after V-J Day. There were two exceptional qualities that led to the decision to use D-M as an aircraft storage area. One was the very dry desert climate; the other was the soil.

The soil, or caliche as it is called, is very hard and able to support the weight of an airplane. It is also an alkaline soil which aids in deterring corrosion. These factors led the USAAF to decide that Davis-Monthan was the perfect spot to store the thousands of aircraft returning from Europe and the Pacific.

During the 1950s most of these surplus aircraft were sold for their aluminum. Scrappers lined the fences of the base with guillotines and smelting furnaces and America's once proud warplanes were reduced to aluminum ingots.

In 1965, the unnamed storage area was designated the Military Aircraft Storage and Disposition Center (MASDC). MASDC's mission was to store Department of Defense aircraft. Besides storage,

Rows of Boeing B-52 bombers in storage at Davis-Monthan during 1982. There are a number of aircraft without nose sections; these were removed to be modified as B-52 cockpit simulators. (U.S. Air Force)

A row of Army Hughes TH-55 Osage two seat light training helicopters parked in the arrivals area at Davis-Monthan. All the aircraft have had their rotor blades removed. (Wonderly)

A Douglas C-124C Globemaster II of the 165th Military Airlift Group, Georgia Air National Guard. Most of the C-124 fleet were retired during the early 1970s and scrapped a short time later. (McKean)

During 1971, a number of C-97s and C-124s arrived at the Davis-Monthan MASDC yard. These aircraft remained in storage for several years undergoing parts reclaimation before they were finally disposed. (U.S. Air Force)

These Douglas RB-66s Destroyers were being readied to return to active duty in Southeast Asia. MASDC was quite active during the Vietnam War providing both aircraft and parts to the war zone. (USAF)

A Convair B-58 Hustler, stripped of its engines and all other usable parts, awaits scrapping during 1975. Most B-58s were retired from the active inventory by 1970. (Weidner)

MASDC personnel would process and maintain the aircraft, perform routine inspections, reclaim aircraft parts (as well as whole aircraft), supply parts for special projects and prepare aircraft for flight.

During the Vietnam War, MASDC supplied 645 aircraft back to the active inventory. Aircraft such as A-3B Skywarriors, F-9 Cougars, RF-8 Crusaders, C-46 Commandos, B-57 Canberras, B-66 Destroyers and C-47s were all returned to the active inventory. As the war wound down, these combat veterans once again returned to MASDC to await further assignment.

MASDC'S mission finally evolved into that of the regeneration of both aircraft and aircraft parts. Additionally, they also maintained a similar facility in California at Norton Air Force Base as a storage area for Atlas, Thor and Titan II missiles and rocket engines. In order to accommodate this ever changing role and to end the boneyard image, a new name was chosen for the facility and in 1985 the center was renamed the Aerospace Maintenance and Regeneration Center (AMARC).

AMARC consists of 2,300 acres enclosed by thirteen miles of perimeter fence line. It houses some 2,500 aircraft as well as a host of rework, preservation, inspection, crating and office buildings. AMARC provides employment to 600 civilian and three full time military personnel.

This facility is unique in that there are at least seventy different aircraft types in one location. AMARC is even more unique in that it actually makes money. For example, for every fiscal 1987 taxpayer dollar spent, AMARC earned $12.00. The total value of aircraft and parts returned to the Department of Defense inventory during FY87 was reported as $271 million.

A T-38 Talon of the 14th Flying Training Wing from Columbus AFB, Mississippi, shares the ramp with another visiting T-38, a pair of Marine A-4Ms and an A-7 Corsair II. D-M is a popular cross-country stop-over location. (Wonderly)

A visiting Marine Corps VH-53D Sikorsky Sea Stallion parked on the D-M transit ramp. The aircraft usually carries journalists and presidential staff members when not being used to transport senior Marine officers. (Wonderly)

With the Mexican border only sixty miles from Tucson, the U.S. Customs Department has surveillance aircraft based at D-M. This Blackhawk is one of the few helicopters that can fly with some twin engined drug running aircraft. (Wonderly)

An A-10A Thunderbolt II of the 355 Tactical Training Wing on the ramp at Davis-Monthan AFB. Pilots have been training in the A-10 at D-M since 1976 and the wing trains over 200 A-10 pilots a year for assignment to operational squadrons. (Wonderly)

This OA-37 Dragonfly of the 23rd Tactical Air Support Squadron was stationed at Davis-Monthan. This unit has since converted to the OA-10 Forward Air Controller (FAC) version of the Republic A-10 Thunderbolt II. (Wonderly)

One of the almost 6,000 North American Sabre Jets built between 1948 and 1956 rests on its tail on the desert floor during 1972. This F-86 was obviously used as a source of spare parts to keep other Sabres flying. (McKean)

U.S. Customs impounded this Douglas C-118 freighter for illegal drug running. The Davis-Monthan based U.S. Customs unit is very busy because of Tucson's close proximity to the Mexican border. (Wonderly)

The Lockheed T-33 was replaced in frontline service with the USAF by the T-38 Talon. AMARC is home to many of the versatile Lockheed trainers, among them aircraft 28 of the Florida Air National Guard. (Wonderly)

One of the more unique ex-military aircraft at D-M is this P-3A Orion of the U.S. Customs Service. The aircraft was turned over to Customs by the Navy and is used to fly border patrol over the Southwest U.S. (Dunham)

This F-4C Phantom II of the Arkansas Air National Guard arrived at AMARC during the Spring of 1987. The F-4C evolved from the Navy F-4B and was originally designated the F-110A. (Wonderly)

This T-33 (57-0563) of the 21st TFW will probably not go through the entire preservation routine. Most T-33s just get their intakes covered and have blocks of wood securing the control surfaces. Normally, T-33s are quickly sold to small air forces worldwide. (Wonderly)

One of two A-7B Corsair IIs that arrived at AMARC on 12 September 1986, from NAS Alameda, California. This aircraft had been assigned to Reserve Carrier Air Wing 30 which was converting to the A-7E. (Wonderly)

The delivery pilot makes final checks on the second CVWR-30 A-7B that arrived at AMARC on 12 September 1986. The Corsair II was painted in a low vis tactical Gray camouflage. (Wonderly)

Preparation

Whether an aircraft is to be stored for a lengthy period or a short one, the process begins with the preservation ritual. The first step in this ordered sequence is to remove the guns, ejection seat charges, classified equipment and any item that could end up as a souvenir.

From there the aircraft is moved on to what is affectionately known as the "Flush Farm." At the "Flush Farm" the fuel is drained and the fuel lines are then pumped full of lightweight oil, then drained again. This process leaves a thin coat of oil in the lines that protects the fuel system.

Once the internal areas are protected, attention is turned to the aircraft exterior. Each aircraft is washed down with a solvent to remove dirt, oil, etc., to prepare it for taping. Engine intakes, exhausts and any other gaps or cracks on the upper airframe are covered and taped; then Spraylat is applied to all openings on the uppersurfaces and fuselage sides.

Spraylat is a vinyl plastic coating that serves several purposes. First, it prohibits the intrusion of dust and moisture. Secondly, it provides protection from sand blasting of the canopies by blowing dirt and dust. Thirdly, Spraylat acts to control the internal temperature of the aircraft. The internal temperature of an unprotected aircraft can reach 200 degrees Fahrenheit causing deterioration to rubber parts, plastic, fabric, and delicate electronic equipment. By using the Spraylat process, internal temperatures raise only 5 degrees above the outside temperature. All openings on the underside of the aircraft, (gear doors, bomb bay doors, etc.) are left open to prevent condensation within the aircraft.

Spraylat is applied with high pressure air through a spray gun. Black Spraylat is applied first and then White Spraylat is sprayed on top. Two coats of each are applied with ample time allowed for each to dry between coats. Before the canopy is sprayed, two small gooseneck tubes are placed between the canopy and the frame, one on each side. These tubes allow the cockpit area to breathe. Average time to complete the Spraylat procedure on an F-4 is between 32 and 40 hours.

During late 1986 a new preservation technique made its appearance — an airplane "baggie." This extra large plastic bag completely encloses the airframe with the same results as the Spraylat. The bag is essentially in three pieces with two zip-lock type closures that run radially around the aircraft.

Two big advantages of the bag are its ability to be reused and the ability to quickly gain access inside of the aircraft at any time. Once Spraylat is applied, it is on permanently and a great deal of effort is required to remove it. From time to time access is needed to the interior of the aircraft. The bag allows unlimited access with just a zip to restore its protective qualities. With Spraylat there is only a one time access; then the Spraylat must be reapplied. Currently, the bag is being tested as an alternative to Spraylat on small aircraft. Larger bombers and transports are not planned to be bagged.

Once the Spraylat or bag has been applied, the aircraft is towed to its storage site under the hot Arizona sun where she will wait for her next duty.

This very weathered Marine F-4S Phantom is having its fuel system purged and flushed with light oil. All unit markings have been over painted and the AMARC ID number has been stenciled on just behind the radome. (Wonderly)

A C-130A Hercules of the New York Air National Guard in the process of having its turbine engines removed. The engines are placed in sealed metal canisters that serve both for storage and shipment. (Wonderly)

This Marine Corps A-6E of VMA (AW)-224 has a large wooden plank across the vertical stabilizer and rudder to secure the rudder. Boards are put on all control surfaces to keep them from banging in the wind. (Wonderly)

An F-4 and an CH-53 Sea Stallion on the preparation ramp awaiting a solvent wash. This washing uses a solvent designed to inhibit corrosion. At this time any active corrosion is treated and the aircraft is fully lubricated. When the aircraft dries it is towed to the Spraylat area. (Wonderly)

An A-7 Corsair II in the process of being "demilitarized." All classified and sensitive instruments, guns, ejection seat charges, and any potential "souvenirs" are removed. The number on the nose is the AMARC identification number. (Wonderly)

Fresh from a complete overhaul, this C-130 is being prepared for storage. The aircraft is parked at the "Flush Farm" where her fuel system is purged with lightweight oil to prevent corrosion. (Wonderly)

One of the over 600 civilian workers at AMARC applies Spraylat to an F-4. He is applying the first of two coats of White. Two coats of Black were previously applied and allowed to dry thoroughly. The entire procedure takes between 32 and 40 hours (for the F-4). (Wonderly)

A Marine Corps AV-8A Harrier, formerly of VMA-231, undergoes the initial taping prior to the application of spraylat. All uppersurface openings are sealed with tape before Spraylat is applied. (Dunham)

Spraylat requires some heavyduty spray equipment to apply it. This Phantom is about to be sprayed with the first of two coats of White Spraylat over the already cured Black Spraylat. (Wonderly)

This highly polished Navy C-131F Samaritan awaits her immediate fate — the Spraylat gun. The aircraft had been formerly assigned to the Commander In Chief Atlantic Fleet (CINCLANTFLT) as a VIP transport. (Dunham)

This CH-47 Chinook has been completely sealed and is parked in its storage spot. All markings have been painted over except the service designation, United States Army. (Dunham)

All of the uppersurface openings on this P-3's fuselage, engine nacelles and wings have been taped and coated with Spraylat. The landing gear wells remain open to prevent condensation from building up within the aircraft. (Wonderly)

A C-131B of the 186th FIS has just completed the preservation process and has the nosewheel tow bar connected as it awaits a tow to the final storage area. (Dunham)

This ex-Coast Guard H-65 Dolphin helicopter has been entirely encased in Spraylat to form a totally sealed cocoon. (Wonderly)

The two flexible tubes protruding from the canopy center section on this T-28 Trojan allows the cockpit to breathe under the Spraylat sealant. This cuts down on condensation within the aircraft. (Wonderly)

This Phantom wears the latest in corrosion protection: a plastic bag. The advantages of the bag are the ease of application, multiple access to the aircraft, and it is reusable. (Dunham)

This large covered working area affords welcomed relief from the blistering Arizona sun for maintenance personnel. A pair of Massachusetts Air National Guard F-106 Delta Darts are receiving their initial preparations for storage. (Dunham)

Patience

It is hot, dry and the sun beats down unmercifully. Row after row after row of once proud aircraft sit and wait in this environment, preserved for their next call to duty. Some will one day be returned to the inventory, others will serve foreign owners, while others may be auctioned off to private owners. A few will be donated to museums to educate and inspire the young.

Due to obsolescence, corrosion, etc., some will surrender their useful parts until they are put to final rest in the smelter's furnace. For whatever the outcome, the aircraft at AMARC wait patiently.

F-102As served with the Idaho Air National Guard from 1964 until being replaced by RF-4Cs during 1975. This particular aircraft was part of a preservation test at D-M, serving as the "control" aircraft, receiving no type of preservation. She took a beating from the elements. (Dunham)

An F-4C Phantom II formerly of the 123rd Fighter Interceptor Squadron, Oregon Air National Guard awaits the preservation process on the D-M ramp. As hydraulic pressure bled off, the flaps and slats have drooped. (Wonderly)

This C-119L was one of the very last of the Flying Boxcars. The C-119L was the last C-119 update and these flew into the mid-1970s. Today there are only five remaining at AMARC and these serve as a source of spare parts. (Wonderly)

A fully preserved EKA-3B Skywarrior of VAQ-135 Ravens. This is the electronic warfare/tanker variant of the A-3B and was affectionately known as "The Whale." The Skywarrior was the heaviest aircraft to ever serve on a carrier deck. (Dunham)

This stripped airframe was one of the original F-111 Aardvark prototypes. (Dunham)

Under a program to refurbish A-6 Intruders at AMARC, this overhauled A-6E is about ready to rejoin the fleet. She had been originally assigned to VA-176 Thunderbolts before her overhaul. (Wonderly)

Still in her Blue and Gold markings, this A-4F Skyhawk (BuNo 154180) served as Blue Angels No. 4 and flew the slot position until 1987. (Wonderly)

This A-4B (BuNo 142772) carries a double identity. Superimposed on the bright Red UH tail code is a large 7V indicating that she was last assigned to a naval reserve unit stationed at NAS Glenview, Illinois. (Wonderly)

This Marine F-4S (BuNo 155767) of VMFAT-101 arrived at AMARC from MCAS Yuma, Arizona. The Sharpshooters were the last Marine Corps F-4 replacement training unit. (Wonderly)

This A3D/A-3B Skywarrior of VAH-10 served with the squadron during the 1960s. All but four of the VAH squadrons (2,4,8,10) were converted to RVAH squadrons flying RA-5C Vigilantes. (Dunham)

This Air Force AC-130A was formerly assigned to the 711th SOS, Air Force Reserve based at Duke Field, Eglin AFB, Florida. During the Vietnam conflict this aircraft had flown with the 16th SOS at Ubon RTAFB, Thailand. The 16th SOS was known as "The Fabulous Four Engine Fighters." (Dunham)

There are a large number of Convair F-106s at AMARC making it one of the most numerous fighters at the facility. The F-106B was the two seat combat proficiency trainer variant of the Delta Dart. (Dunham)

These AV-8A Harriers of VMA-542 Flying Tigers are fully preserved for long term storage. The Marines have replaced the AV-8A with the improved AV-8B Super Harrier. (Wonderly)

The T-34B Mentor and VT-1 are both part of Navy history now. The T-34B has been replaced by the turbine powered T-34C. After 35 hours in the Turbo Mentor, prospective naval aviators move on to the T-2 Buckeye. (Wonderly)

There are less than a dozen Douglas C-47 Skytrains still at AMARC and these are probably the oldest of the type in the inventory. Aircraft 662 was formerly assigned to the Continental Air Command. (Dunham)

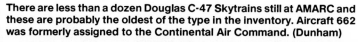

Still carrying its shark mouth, this Marine Corps McDonnell-Douglas TAV-8 Harrier has been placed in long term storage. With the introduction of newer AV-8B Harriers most of the older AV-8As are in storage. (Wonderly)

During 1987, the 159th FIS of the 125th FIG, Florida Air National Guard became the first Air Guard unit to convert to the F-16. With this conversion, the unit flew their F-106 Delta Darts to D-M for storage. (Dunham)

A Lockheed T-33A Shooting Star of the D.C. Air National Guard. Many retired Shooting Stars will find their way to Mexico to become front line equipment once more. The intakes are sealed with foil and Spraylat has not yet been applied. (Wonderly)

This stripped and weathered RA-4C Vigilante will probably be scrapped in the near future. The Vigilante has been retired from active service for a number of years and has been replaced by TARPS F-14s and RF-18 Hornets. (Wonderly)

From three to four North American F-100 Super Sabres were prepared for drone duty on a monthly basis. This particular Super Sabre went through the program during February of 1988. (Wonderly)

This Roman-nosed Lockheed C-130A Hercules is unmistakable even under the coats of Spraylat. The aircraft still carries its Southeast Asia camouflage scheme. (Wonderly)

These salvaged wing panels from a Lockheed T-33A Shooting Star have been crated for shipment as replacement parts for a T-33 somewhere in the world. (Wonderly)

In a program to extend the life of the KC-135 fleet, the Air Force bought a number of 707s, removed the engines and horizontal stabilizers and installed them on KC-135Es. Excess parts were sold to civil 707 operators. The government bought the aircraft for $1 million each and reclaimed some $12 million in parts. (Wonderly)

The Grumman TF-9J Cougar was used by the Navy as an advanced fighter-trainer during the 1960s. This TF-9J (BuNo 147383) was formerly flown by VT-25 and still carries her high visibility Orange markings. (Dunham)

The Los Angeles Dodgers' Boeing 707 team aircraft was one of the 707s that was stripped for the KC-135E rebuild program. All KC-135Es are assigned to Air Force Reserve and Air National Guard units. (Wonderly)

The Navy has two Reserve Carrier Air Wings (CVWRs) and this LTV A-7B Corsair II was formerly flown by CVWR-30 based at NAS Miramar, California. (Wonderly)

This F-4N Phantom II (BuNo 150484) of VMFA-323 Death Rattlers was based at MCAS El Toro. VMFA-323 flew more than 100,000 combat sorties during the Vietnam war. (Wonderly)

A pair of F-4 Phantoms completely sealed in huge plastic bags. Currently the bags are used only for smaller aircraft. Bombers and transports are not bagged. (Wonderly)

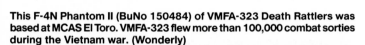

This CH-53A Sea Stallion came to AMARC during the Spring of 1987 after severe corrosion grounded the aircraft. She was one of the first Sea Stallions to be transferred to AMARC. (Dunham)

There are not many F-101B Voodoos left in the yard, since most were scrapped long ago. This F-101B formerly served with the Texas Air National Guard and still has the Texans logo on the fuselage. (Wonderly)

Two ex-USAF C-130s were transferred to the Navy as DC-130A Drone Directors. They were flown by Composite Squadron Three (VC-3), based at NAS North Island, San Diego, California until they were retired and sent to AMARC. (Wonderly)

The Republic F-105 Thunderchief saw twenty-five years of service with the USAF. The F-105D was the most numerous variant and this one last flew with the 121st TFS of the D.C. Air National Guard. A number of "Thuds" from AMARC have gone to museums. (Dunham)

Heavy Layers of White Spraylat cover this F-4C Phantom of the California Air National Guard. Most of the USAF Phantoms have entered AMARC configured with both wing and centerline fuel tanks. (Wonderly)

During 1966, the USAF purchased 346 Cessna Super Skymasters as replacements for the Cessna O-1 Bird Dog. The O-2 FAC aircraft more than proved itself in Southeast Asia. The last unit to fly the O-2 was based at Shaw AFB, S.C. (Wonderly)

The SP-2H Neptune entered service during 1947 and served into the 1960s, seeing combat in Vietnam. This SP-2H last served with VP-67 at NAS Millington, Tenn. VP-67 was the last patrol squadron to fly the Neptune, transitioning to the P-3 during 1979. (Dunham)

An F-4C Phantom of the 123rd Tactical Fighter Squadron, Oregon Air National Guard parked on the hard desert at AMARC. This unit had several F-4s that were credited with MiG kills. (Wonderly)

This McDonnell-Douglas F-101B Voodoo interceptor has had the landing gear, canopy, engines and a host of other parts removed to supply spares for other Voodoos. (Dunham)

A Florida Air National Guard T-33A (52-9803) parked in the grassy storage area with a number of other T-33s. These aircraft will not go through the full preservation procedure since they will be quickly sold to countries such as Mexico. (Dunham)

The Rockwell A3J Vigilante was reconfigured from an attack bomber to a high speed reconnaissance aircraft designated the RA-5C. The last RA-5C squadron, RVAH-7, was decommissioned during September of 1979, at NAS Key West. (Wonderly)

A Marine F-4J (BuNo 153777) of VMFAT-101. The faded SH tail code identifies the Phantom as having been assigned to VMFAT-101 Sharp-shooters, the Marine Phantom training unit based at MCAS Yuma. (Dunham)

17

A lineup of Convair F-106 Delta Darts of California Air National Guard, Florida Air National Guard, 95th FIS, 5th FIS, 87th FIS, and Montana Air National Guard. (Kula)

An F-4C Phantom II of the 199th FIS, Hawaii Air National Guard. The HANG, based at Hickam Field, has replaced their F-4Cs with F-15A/B Eagles. The Hawaiian aircraft sport an Orange and Red wave style fin stripe. (Wonderly)

A Lockheed T-33A Shooting Star formerly of the 5th FIS Spittin' Kittens based at Minot Air Force Base, North Dakota. Over 6,500 Shooting Stars were built in the U.S., Canada and Japan. (Dunham)

An overall Black Martin B-57C Canberra of the Vermont Air National Guard. The Green Mountain Boys were the last unit to fly the B-57. B-57s were often modified by removing all weapons equipment and adding ECM gear and an Electronic Warfare Officer (EWO). (Wonderly)

This stripped General Dynamics F-111A Aardvark has been at AMARC since the mid-1970s. The aircraft was built during 1965 and was used primarily as a test vehicle. (Wonderly)

The Coast Guard used the Convair C-131A for medium range search and rescue and law enforcement. They designated these ex-USAF aircraft HC-131As. This aircraft, one of twenty in service, retained the SAC band around the fuselage. (Wonderly)

This Boeing B-52D Stratofortress formerly served with the 22nd Bomb Wing and saw combat during the Vietnam war. The aircraft still carries its Southeast Asia style camouflage. (Dunham)

An early Lockheed NC-130A Hercules test aircraft of the ASD (Aeronautical Systems Division). This USAF unit carries out a number of different test functions including: weather research, missile tracking/recovery and air sampling. (Wonderly)

Red marker cones around this Hawaii Air National Guard F-4C Phantom warn of work in progress. The stand under the nose enables workers to safely remove parts or do repair work in the nosewheel area. (Dunham)

This Convair F-106B Delta Dart was formerly assigned to the 49th FIS based at Griffiss AFB, New York. The QF-106 is replacing the QF-100, QF-106 advantages include supersonic speed and increased maneuverability. (Wonderly)

This F-100F Super Sabre formerly of the 152nd Tactical Fighter Training Wing, Arizona ANG, will be converted to the QF-100 drone configuration. Pilots at a recent William Tell competition knocked out nine QF-100Ds. To prolong the life of these $400,000 aircraft, technicians have installed propane pods on the wing tips to draw heat seeking missiles away from the tail pipe. (Dunham)

This McDonnell-Douglas F-101B Voodoo interceptor of the 132nd FIS Maine Air National Guard has had the main landing gear removed and is resting on wooden work stands. (Kula)

This Republic F-105 Thunderchief is parked in the materials testing area where aircraft and helicopters are used to test preservation paints, coatings and tapes. (Dunham)

An overall Black Vermont Air National Guard Martin B-57C. The aircraft was last operated by a Defense Systems Evaluation Squadron (DSES) in the electronic aggressor role probing U.S. air defenses. (Dunham)

As part of the QF-100 program, major rework is done on each F-100 Super Sabre before it flies in the drone configuration. Most QF-100s are ex-Air National Guard aircraft and carry Southeast Asia camouflage. (Wonderly)

A U.S. Army Sikorsky H-34 Choctaw helicopter sits patiently alongside several SH-34J Sea Bats (Navy H-34s). There are only half a dozen H-34s remaining in AMARC's inventory. (Dunham)

A Hawaii Air National Guard F-4C Phantom parked in the arrival area alongside a USMC CH-53 Sea Stallion. Both are recent arrivals and neither aircraft has begun the preservation process. (Wonderly)

There are over 100 North American T-39 Sabreliner light transports stored at AMARC. The T-39 has been replaced in USAF service by the C-21A Learjet. (Wonderly)

This F-4D Phantom of the 136th FIS, New York Air National Guard was formerly based at Niagra Falls. The average age of Air National Guard Phantoms arriving at AMARC is twenty years. (Dunham)

This overall White McDonnell-Douglas A-4L Skyhawk carries Blue flight test colors. A number of different variants of the A-4 have been removed from AMARC and sold to both Singapore and Malaysia. (Dunham)

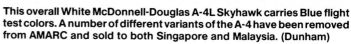

The transit ramp at D-M usually has a variety of aircraft parked on it. Four T-38 Talons and three T-37s await the return of their students to begin another leg of their cross-country training flight. (Wonderly)

Sensitive areas such as wing leading edges, radar pods and antenna are often completely covered with Spraylat, such as on this Army OV-1 Mohawk reconnaissance aircraft. (Wonderly)

The B-52 force in storage at AMARC is still considered part of our strategic inventory. Until recently, the Soviets reportedly photographed the yard via satellite periodically to keep track of the B-52s. (Wonderly)

A USAF Northrop T-38 Talon rests on props after its main landing gear were removed. During the last twenty-five years, more than 56,999 U.S. and NATO pilots have been trained on the T-38. (Wonderly)

Assigned to the role of electronic bandits for NORAD exercises, this EB-57E was flown by the 17th Defense Evaluation Squadron out of Malsltrom AFB, Montana. The vent tubes on top of the cockpit are for venting internal heat. (Wonderly)

Under a program called *Pacer Six*, the Air Force will convert nearly 200 Convair F-106 Delta Darts into hIgh performance drones under the designation QF-106. The QF-106 drones will be used by the Air Force and Army as aerial targets. (Wonderly)

The 58th Weather Reconnaissance Squadron at Kirkland AFB, New Mexico, operated the WB-57F before it went into storage. This aircraft made routine flights above 60,000 feet for air sampling and other weather research. (Dunham)

All USAF Fairchild C-123 Providers were transferred to the Air Force Reserve before they were finally retired to AMARC. These aircraft can be purchased by civil owners under the civilian use plan.

The Grumman OV-1 Mohawk continues to serve the U.S. Army in the battlefield surveillance role and late model OV-1s saw action during Operation DESERT STORM. There are some fifty Mohawks in storage, mostly earlier OV-1A and OV-1B variants. (Wonderly)

These Convair F-106 Delta Darts of the 102nd FIW, Massachusetts ANG, were replaced by McDonnell-Douglas F-15A Eagles. This unit was one of the last to ferry their F-106s to AMARC. (Wonderly)

An ex-Reserve RF-8G Crusader on the ramp at AMARC. Normally, the RF-8s arrive at the center with all of their former unit markings and codes removed. The numbers on the nose are center identification numbers. (Wonderly)

A preserved F-4N Phantom II (BuNo 151482), formerly of Marine Fighter Attack Squadron (VMFA) 112, the Cowboys. The unit was one of two Marine Reserve F-4N squadrons based at NAS Dallas. (Wonderly)

This F-100D Super Sabre has been converted for use as a target drone. Before the aircraft leaves the center, all systems are brought up to standard, checked out and the aircraft is test flown. (Dunham)

An F-106A of the 101st Fighter Interceptor Squadron, Massachusettes Air National Guard on the ramp during February of 1988. The 101st FIS received its first F-106s during June of 1972. (Wonderly)

25

The Grumman OV-1 Mohawk carried an eighteen foot fiberglass Side Looking Airborne Radar (SLAR) pod on the starboard side. SLAR was used extensively in Southeast Asia to track enemy movements. (Wonderly)

The P-3 Orion entered service during 1963, and seems to still have a long future ahead of it. This Orion is a relatively rare TP-3A (BuNo 151359l) crew trainer. (Wonderly)

Some aircraft are immediately marked for parts reclaimation/scrapping as evidenced by the bright Red Disposal under the word Coast on this HH-52A Sikorsky Seaguard. Whether due to corrosion or high time on the airframe, this helicopter has made its last flight. (Dunham)

This F-4N Phantom of VF-21 carries the NK tail code it carried while flying off USS CORAL SEA. VF-21 Freelancers made three Vietnam combat cruises with the Phantom flying off USS MIDWAY, CORAL SEA and RANGER. (Wonderly)

A rather weathered and tired looking DC-130A Hercules drone director rests on the hard desert sand. The aircraft carries the early three blade propellers used on C-130As. (Wonderly)

Entering service as the F8U-1P during 1958, this photo Crusader was redesignated as an RF-8A during 1962. In 1965, some seventy-three RF-8As were rebuilt as RF-8Gs and on 30 March 1987, the RF-8G made its last scheduled military flight. (Wonderly)

This Douglas C-118 was formerly operated by VR-54, a Naval Reserve transport squadron based at NAS New Orleans. The venerable Liftmaster was replaced by the McDonnell-Douglas C-9A Skytrain II. (Wonderly)

The first unit to fly the Phantom in USMC service was the Gray Ghosts of VMFA-531. This unit received its first Phantoms during June of 1962, when it was assigned duty at NAS Key West during the Cuban Missile crisis. VMFA-531 was also the first to fly the Phantom in Vietnam, being based at Danang during 1965. (Wonderly)

A JC-130B Hercules of the Air Force Systems Command. The JC-130 was used during the *Falling Star* program and would snag packages jettisoned from orbiting satellites. Normally, five aircraft would be involved on each mission. (Dunham)

A Marine Corps AH-1J Sea Cobra. The AH-1J is being replaced in active Marine squadrons by the improved AH-1W. Marine Cobras differ from Army aircraft in having twin P&W T-400 turbine engines. (Wonderly)

This partially stripped F-104D was formerly assigned to the Puerto Rican Air National Guard, the last Air Force unit to operate the Starfighter. The F-104s served from 1967 through July of 1975, when they were replaced by A-7Ds. (Dunham)

A cocooned F-4N Phantom II of VFMA-531. The F-4N was a rebuilt and upgraded variant of the F-4B Phantom II, the first production variant of the Phantom. The last F-4Ns were retired from service during 1990. (Dunham)

Nancy was a C-118 formerly flown by VR-24 out of NAS New Orleans. Navy Reserve VR squadrons, like VR-24, provide airlift support for both Reserve and active forces with C-9 Transports. (Dunham)

A wooden plank secures the rudder on this A-6E Intruder, formerly flown by Marine All Weather Attack Squadron (VMA AW) 224. Marines operate Intruders in the all weather attack role. (Wonderly)

This CH-46E Seaknight arrived at the facility during early 1988. The aircraft was formerly flown by HMM-266. The Marines have a long history with the CH-46, having first introduced the aircraft into service during Vietnam. (Dunham)

A very clean and well maintained F-4C Phantom II of the Arkansas Air National Guard. This unit has since converted to the F-16. (Wonderly)

This is the Sikorsky YSH-60B Seahawk anti-submarine/anti-ship helicopter prototype. Prototype test aircraft often spend time at AMARC between test programs or awaiting modification. (Wonderly)

This EP-2H Neptune (BuNo 148343) carries Red and Yellow drone controller markings. The tail code GF indicates that this Neptune served with the Redtails of VC-8 based at Roosevelt Roads, Puerto Rico. (Wonderly)

A Republic F-105G Wild Weasel of the 35th Tactical Fighter Wing. The aircraft carries a variation of the Southeast Asia style camouflage. Spraylat has been applied to all uppersurface openings. (Wonderly)

This F-100 will be converted to a full-scale aerial target (FSAT) QF-100 drone. Aircraft like this ex-Indiana Air National Guard F-100D save the government a great deal of money in training pilots in air-to-air gunnery. (Wonderly)

A dual control, side-by-side seat Convair TF-102 Delta Dagger combat proficiency trainer of the 190th FIS, Idaho Air National Guard. There were a total of 111 TF-102s built. (Wonderly)

A Convair F-106A Delta Dart formerly of the 125th Fighter Interceptor Group, Florida Air National Guard, based at Jacksonville, Fla. There are large numbers of F-106s at AMARC. (Wonderly)

Several heavy layers of Spraylat were applied to provide adequate protection for the large glass windshield of this USMC UH-1 Huey. There is a small aluminum vent tube protruding from the side window. (Wonderly)

This Northrop T-38A Talon of the 26th Tactical Fighter Training Squadron carries an early aggressor paint scheme. T-38s and F-5s were used to simulate the Soviet MiG-21 Fishbed fighter. (Wonderly)

The Red lightning bolt on the tail identifies this F-4S Phantom II as being assigned to VF-161 Chargers. The F-4S was a rebuilt F-4J with wing slats and upgraded avionics. (Wonderly)

An E-2B Hawkeye (BuNo 150539) parked on the receiving ramp during September of 1986. The E-2B, which entered service during 1960, has been replaced in active squadrons by the improved E-2C. This Hawkeye had been flown by VAW-88 out of NAS Miramar, California. (Wonderly)

This F-106A Delta Dart of the 186th Fighter Interceptor Squadron, Montana Air National Guard, will soon be re-built as a drone. These former ANG F-106s have been selected to be modified as high speed target drones. (Wonderly)

This OV-10A Bronco was assigned to the 27th TASS at George Air Force Base, California, before being retired to the facility. The Bronco saw widespread service over Vietnam and Marine OV-10s saw service during Operation DESERT STORM. (Wonderly)

A TAV-8A Harrier of VMAT-203. This TAV-8 was a two place trainer used to transition pilots of conventional aircraft into the vertical takeoff Harrier. The TAV-8 was also used as a "Fast FAC" forward air control aircraft. (Dunham)

A former Marine F-4J Phantom II of VFMA-312, Checkerboards. The aircraft was based at MCAS Beaufort, South Carolina, known to Marines as "Phantom Town." VFMA-312 was the last active Marine Phantom unit and has since converted to the F/A-18 Hornet. (Dunham)

Originally designated the TF-1, the C-1A Trader served as a carrier onboard delivery (COD) aircraft with VR squadrons. Normally, each carrier had a C-1A assigned as the ship's aircraft. A total of eighty-seven C-1As were built. (Wonderly)

An NA-3B Skywarrior (BuNo 138938) of the Pacific Missile Test Center, Point Mugu, California. The N in the aircraft's designator identified it as being assigned to the permanent special test role. (Wonderly)

The Fairchild Republic T-46A was designed to replace the aging Cessna T-37 trainer, but the program was cancelled. Three prototypes were completed, partially tested, then sent to AMARC for storage. (Dunham)

Navy and Marine Corps Phantoms are rapidly being joined by Air Force variants such as this Phantom of the Texas Air National Guard. The advent of newer fighters such as the F-16 and F-15 has accelerated the retirement of the F-4. (Wonderly)

A Lockheed VC-140B Jetstar of the 1254th Special Air Missions Unit, Andrews AFB, Washington, D. C. Only a handful of the original sixteen Jetstars are still in active service. Military Airlift Command uses the aircraft to evaluate landing systems, NAV aids and radar approach equipment. (Wonderly)

The Fairchild C-123 Provider began as a Second World War glider project. After many years of service with TAC and AFRes units, the C-123s were replaced by C-130s. The last military flight was during 1986 when a UC-123K aerial sprayer was delivered to AMARC. (Dunham)

At one time there was a drone controller squadron stationed at Davis-Monthan that flew drone controller C-130s like this DC-130A. The Hercules was formerly attached to the 4950th Test Wing of the Aeronautical Systems Division at Wright Patterson AFB, Ohio. (Dunham)

There are hundreds of Boeing B-52 Stratofortress bombers stored at AMARC. The B-52 has remained operational longer than any bomber in U.S. military history and one of the reasons was the parts that these stored aircraft have supplied to frontline squadrons. (Dunham)

The Sikorsky H-34 saw service with all four branches of the U.S. military. This overall Orange Navy SH-34J Seahorse flew with Helicopter Training Squadron Eight, HT-8. The Navy retired the SH-34J in the late 1960s. (Wonderly)

This F-4J Phantom II was formerly attached to the Naval Air Test Center (NATC) and carried the tail code 7T. A total of 522 F-4Js were built for the U.S. Navy and Marine Corps with the first being delivered during 1966. (Wonderly)

This Beechcraft U-8 Seminole light transport served with the Nebraska National Guard. The engine has been uncovered and will probably be stripped to provide parts for another aircraft. (Wonderly)

Less than a dozen Convair F-102 Delta Daggers remain in storage. The majority that were not scrapped were converted to the QF-102 aerial target drones. This F-102 carries Southeast Asia style camouflage. (Wonderly)

A C-130A of the Montana Air National Guard rests on the hard desert floor after over thirty years of service. The performance and longevity of these aircraft is directly attributed to the care given them by their maintenance crews. (Dunham)

These Northrop T-38A Talons have been prepared for crating and shipment. The boxes behind the aircraft contain delicate parts which are specially packaged and will be placed inside the aircraft crate. (Wonderly)

A partially stripped Boeing RB-47 Stratojet formerly of the Strategic Air Command. This RB-47 is one of two still residing at AMARC. Most of the B-47 fleet was scrapped on the center grounds and the parts sold to recyclers. (Puzzullo)

Partially stripped for usable parts, this F-111A previously served with the Air Force Systems Command. The F-111 prototype made its first flight during 1964 and F-111Es were among the first strike aircraft into Iraq during Operation DESERT STORM. (Dunham)

This Republic F-105B was formerly operated by the 141st Tactical Fighter Squadron, New Jersey Air National Guard. This aircraft was saved and is now on display at the Pima Air Museum, Tucson, Arizona. (Puzzullo)

A very weathered RB-66B Destroyer, formerly of the 363rd Tactical Reconnaissance Wing. The aircraft was saved and became part of the aircraft collection of the Pima Air Museum in Tucson. (Puzzullo)

This F-100F Super Sabre, at Mojave, was formerly flown by the Missouri Air National Guard. The aircraft has been converted to the QF-100 target drone configuration and carries high visibility markings on the nose and fin. (Puzzullo)

This EC-121 Warning Star was flown by the U.S. Navy at the Pacific Missile Test Center, Point Mugu, California. The aircraft was used to monitor missile tests over the Pacific. (Puzzullo)

An F-4D Phantom II of the 127th Tactical Fighter Training Squadron, Kansas Air National Guard — the Jayhawks. The aircraft was used to train Phantom crews for other tactical fighter squadrons. (Wonderly)

This Boeing 367-80 served as the prototype for the KC-135 Strato-tanker and the 707 commercial jet airliner, although it differed from both in a number of ways. The aircraft had been in storage at the center since 1972, but during the summer of 1991, it was flown to Boeing Field for restoration prior to being returned to the NASM. (Dunham)

This F-4C Phantom of the 111th FIS, Texas Air National Guard was formerly based in Houston. The Texans logo and tail colors are well known in USAF circles and are currently being carried by F-16s. This aircraft is one of the newer USAF Phantoms to enter AMARC. (Wonderly)

This Douglas A3D-1 Skywarrior was loaned to Hughes as a testbed. After years of service the aircraft was placed in storage during 1975. The A-3 was modified with a thimble nose radome. (Wonderly)

An overall Light Gull Gray U.S. Navy Lockheed T2V-2 Seastar. The Seastar was a modified Lockheed T-33 Shooting Star built for the Navy pilot training program. (Wonderly)

This TF-102 carries Southeast Asia camouflage. The aircraft was formerly assigned to the 190th FIS, Idaho Air National Guard. Painted surfaces like the flat Southeast Asian colors fade quickly under the desert sun. (Wonderly)

Phase out of the Lochkeed T-33 Shooting Star as a frontline jet trainer began during 1961 when the T-38 Talon was introduced into service. Since then, T-33s have been used in a variety of second line roles. This T-33A was assigned to the 96th FITS at Tyndall AFB, Florida. (Wonderly)

This overall ADC Gray McDonnell-Douglas F-4C Phantom II was last flown b the 123rd FIS, Oregon Air National Guard. The Phantom next to it was from the New York Air National Guard. (Wonderly)

A Martin WB-57 of NASA's Earth Survey Program. These B-57s were highly modified with new engines and an extended/broadened wing. Originally they were used for reconnaissance missions. (Puzzullo)

This Boeing KC-97L was formerly attached to the 197th Air Refueling Squadron, Arizona Air National Guard, based in Phoenix. The KC-97 tanker fleet served in the Air Guard until their retirement to AMARC in the mid-1970s. Today no KC-97s remain at AMARC. (Puzzullo)

This overall Natural Metal Martin WB-57 Canberra was formerly flown by the 58th Weather Reconnaissance Squadron, Military Airlift Command. The tail band was Black with Yellow lettering and borders. (Puzzullo)

This Grumman US-2B Tracker was the station aircraft from NAF Sigonella. A number of S-2s were removed from AMARC and converted to fire bombers. Some have received turboprop engines and still others serve with foreign navies. (Puzzullo)

This F-4N (BuNo 153914) was last assigned to VF-21 Freelancers aboard USS CORAL SEA. The Black numbers above the squadron identification are the center identification serial number. (Wonderly)

This overall Black F-4S, formerly of VX-4, was preserved during June of 1989. VX-4 is based at Point Mugu, California and this Phantom carried a large White Playboy Bunny marking on the tail at one point during its career. (Dunham)

The Piper PA-48 Enforcer was a turboprop development of the North American P-51 Mustang fighter of WW II and was intended as an alternate to the A-10. The aircraft failed to find a buyer and was placed in storage during 1984. (Dunham)

This former USAF C-118 Liftmaster still has its high visibility Orange markings on the nose. The number on the nose wheel door (CG041) is the center inventory number. (Wonderly)

A sharkmouthed F-4N Phantom formerly of VF-111 Sundowners, based at NAS Miramar, California. This aircraft is now preserved at Luke AFB, Arizona. (Puzzullo)

The North American/Rockwell RA-5C Vigilante was an unarmed reconnaissance version of the A3J/A-5 heavy attack bomber. The RA-5C carried a large array of electronic equipment and cameras in the underfuselage canoe fairing. (Puzzullo)

A Republic RF-84F Thunderflash in Southeast Asia style camouflage. The RF-84F was a photo reconnaissance variant of the F-84F Thunderstreak fighter-bomber. The camera nose could hold as many as six cameras. (Wonderly)

The DHC C-7 Caribou saw considerable service in Vietnam first with the Army and then with the Air Force. The few remaining ex-Air National Guard aircraft can be found within the yard at AMARC or at nearby civilian yards. (Wonderly)

This McDonnell-Douglas RF-101C Voodoo last served with the 165th Tactical Reconnaissance Squadron, Kentucky Air National Guard. (Puzzullo)

This Douglas C-118B Liftmaster was formerly flown by VR-52 (Fleet Logistics Support Squadron Fifty Two) based at NAS Willow Grove, PA. A number of C-118 have been purchased by civil operators and the aircraft is very popular with civilian air freighters. (Puzzullo)

The Grumman C-2 Greyhound was a Carrier Onboard Delivery aircraft based on the E-2 Hawkeye. There are only a few of these aircraft in storage. (Wonderly)

This Lockheed S-3A Viking belonged to VS-41 when it was on active duty. The aircraft was placed in storage at AMARC during 1983, but was later returned to active service. The Viking now flies with VS-22. (Puzzullo)

These three Convair F-102 Delta Daggers were last flown by Air National Guard units. The F-102 has gone through AMARC in large numbers, the majority becoming Sperry PQM-102 target drones. Less than a dozen remain in AMARC today. (Puzzullo)

This Boeing KC-97L was last operated by the 191st Air Refueling Squadron, Utah Air National Guard, based at Salt Lake City. The KC-97 was replaced in Air National Guard units by the KC-135. (Puzzullo)

This Grumman C-1A Trader carries the markings of USS LEXINGTON (CVT-16). The C-1 was assigned as the ship's aircraft and carried two nicknames: *Ghost Rider* on the nacelle and *BLUE GHOST* under the Navy on the fuselage. (Wonderly)

A Vought F-8K Crusader formerly of Marine Fighter Squadron (VMF) 351. A number of F-8s were removed from storage, completely refurbished and sold to the Philippine Air Force. (Puzzullo)

The 119th FIS, 177 FIG, New Jersey Air National Guard was the last unit to retire the F-106A Delta Dart. The Atlantic City based unit now flies the F-16 Fighting Falcon. (Wonderly)

43

This F-4D Phantom was once operated by the 183rd Tactical Fighter Group, Illinois Air National Guard based at Springfield. The tail band is Yellow with the state name (Illinois) in Black. (Wonderly)

This Grumman S-2 Tracker may one day fly again as a fire bomber. A number of S-2s have left the yard after being refurbished as fire bombers, and are owned by the state of California. (Wonderly)

This F-4D from the 160th Tactical Fighter Squadron, Alabama Air National Guard was based at Montgomery. The aircraft carries an unusual upper-surface camouflage of Dark Gray, Medium Green and Brown. (Wonderly)

There are number of early Lockheed P-3 Orions at AMARC. This P-3A was flown by VP-94, at NAS New Orleans. The aircraft is up on blocks indicating that the main landing gear has been removed. (Wonderly)

A number of F-4J Phantoms were rebuilt and modernized under the designation F-4S. This Marine F-4S was last flown by VMFA-321 a Marine Reserve unit stationed at NAF Andrews, Washington, D.C. (Wonderly)

This camouflaged F-4C (63-7704) of the Oregon Air National Guard was credited with a MiG-17 kill during 1967. At that time she was assigned to the 480th TFS, 366th TFW. (Wonderly)

A Convair C-131 formerly of the Montana Air National Guard. This versatile aircraft has disappeared from most of the Air Force and Air Guard units and has been replaced by more modern light transports. (Wonderly)

Air Force F-4 Phantoms have arrived at AMARC in many various paint schemes. This two tone Gray F-4D was from the 160th Tactical Fighter Squadron, Alabama Air National Guard at Montgomery. This color scheme was known as the Egyptian One scheme. (Wonderly)

This Douglas F3D/F-10 Skynight is parked on Museum Row, an area where one aircraft of each type in the yard is displayed. This aircraft was last flown by a Marine unit. (Wonderly)

This Grumman C-1A Trader was the station aircraft assigned to NAS Cecil Field, Florida. The Trader was used to ferry high priority freight and passengers and could carry a payload of 3,500 pounds. (Wonderly)

The high flight hours on the airframe of this Navy Phantom of VF-161, led to it being used as a source of spare parts. Wooden supports, designed and made at AMARC, serve as landing gear, since the originals have been removed. (Wonderly)

An F-105D (60-0504) sits proudly on Museum Row. This Thud downed a MiG-17 in 1967 while assigned to the 333rd TFS, 355th TFW. Her last home before AMARC was with the 121st TFS, D.C. Air National Guard. (Dunham)

A lone T-34C Turbo Mentor of TAW-5 sits on the D-M transient ramp during June of 1989 alongside a line of T-38A Talons from the 12th FTW based at Randolph AFB, Texas. (Dunham)

Except for the missing horizontal stabilizers and fin tip, this RF-101C (56-0115) appears to be in relatively good shape. There were a total of 166 RF-101Cs produced and many saw combat during the Vietnam war. (Dunham)

This C-131D (54-2819) was last assigned to the famous Happy Hooligans, the North Dakota Air National Guard. This Samaritan and most of the unit's F-4s now call AMARC home. (Dunham)

This jet assisted C-123 Provider will probably end up in civilian hands — hopefully not running drugs. A number of C-123s have ended up with the DEA after being repossessed from their drug running owners. (Dunham)

The lead aircraft in this row of Air Force Hueys is a TH-1F (66-1238) trainer. The aircraft was formerly attached to the 405 TTW, Luke AFB, Arizona. The second and third Hueys in line are preserved in plastic bags. (Dunham)

A McDonnell-Douglas A-4M Skyhawk (BuNo 158167) formerly assigned to VMA-214. The A-4M was the last production variant of the Skyhawk and was built specifically for the Marines. VMA-214 traces its line back to VMF-214, the famous Blacksheep Squadron of WW II. (Dunham)

These UH-1 Huey helicopters were modified with especially high landing skids. One rumor has it that the design was to allow for safer landings in low swampy areas like rice paddies. (Dunham)

This was one of two F-106 chase planes used during the B-1 bomber program. This F-106B (57-2535) was originally assigned to the Florida Air National Guard. The tail markings were in Black. (Dunham)

An F-4D of the 170th TFS, Illinois Air National Guard. During early 1972 the 170th TFS became the first Air National Guard Squadron to receive the F-4 Phantom. (Dunham)

During 1975, the Idaho Air National Guard had its mission changed and began flying RF-4C Phantoms. This RF-4C (66-8599) has a Loran antenna array mounted on the fuselage spine. (Dunham)

This F-4D (66-7771) was from the 906th TFG, 89th TFS, at Wright Patterson AFB. The tail code DO identifies the aircraft's home base as Dayton, Ohio. (Dunham)

This overall ADC Gray F-4C (64-9775) previously served with the 114th Tactical Fighter Training Squadron, Oregon Air National Guard. The aircraft is configured with dual Sidewinder missile rails on the inboard wing pylons. (Dunham)

This Navy UH-1L (Buno 157858) has been procured by one of the area's aircraft dealers. It was towed to the Davis-Monthan property line, where it was delivered to her new owner. (Wonderly)

Rows of C-130s, F-4s, B-57s, OV-1s, AV-8s, S-2s, P-3s, and P2Vs occupy just one of the parcels in the 3,000 acre AMARC facility. (Fugere/ AMARC)

Carrying the legend STRIKE on the fuselage below the tail and on the nosewheel door, this A-4B was destined for Singapore but now rests at AMARC. It was formerly stationed at the Naval Air Training Unit, Jacksonville, Florida. (Dunham)

Not all aircraft leave the center in one piece. Blue Angels 3 (A-4F BuNo 154179) was partially disassembled and mounted on pallets for further shipment. The ultimate destination of the Skyhawk is unknown. (Wonderly)

Transition

Change at AMARC is not immediately visible to the unknowing eye but it is always happening. Careful study over a short period of time will reveal that the facility is anything but a burial ground. Regeneration is not only part of the name, it is the best way to describe the activity on the base on a day to day basis.

The circumstances under which an aircraft comes to AMARC are as varied as the aircraft themselves. Some come to the yard with high hours, some for storage awaiting modification, some to be re-processed for export to a foreign government, and some will stay until the new owner, usually a museum, can arrange to move them. The majority of airframes are reserves, surplus or simply outdated.

The status of every aircraft is charted and followed in a control center that resembles the air traffic control center at any major airport. The inventory is monitored and any change recorded whether it be a QF-100 drone leaving for Mojave or a search for a strut part for a Nationalist Chinese HU-16 Albatross.

Parts reclaimation continues to be a major task for AMARC. For instance, AMARC was the first stop in the KC-135E re-engine program. The Air Force purchased more than 150 Boeing 707 airliners, from which AMARC removed the JT3D engines which were then retrofitted to the KC-135E. Many other parts have also been used, including the horizontal stabilizers.

Numerous special repair projects are on-going such as modifying pylons to launch different types of weapons. AMARC returns approximately one half of the stored aircraft to duty and aircraft that will never fly again also fill an important role as a source of parts.

The contingency withdrawal program for the various branches of the military in wartime or other emergencies is one of AMARC's most important functions and over 645 aircraft were removed from storage during the Vietnam conflict.

Although every aircraft could tell a story, there are many that have led especially colorful careers. Until the Summer of 1991, the "Dash 80" (Boeing 707 prototype) was stored there. Other more colorful aircraft have included both of the B-29s that dropped nuclear bombs (*ENOLA GAY* and *BOCKSCAR*), President Truman's *SAC-RED COW* C-54 transport, various Blue Angel and Thunderbird mounts, the Los Angeles Dodgers' 707, the record setting B-58 *PULASKI HUSTLER* and the B-52 mothership for the X-15 program. More recently, there was an HU-16 Albatross which is now being flown on the warbird circuit by the man who flew it while he was in the Navy.

Numerous programs have been cancelled over the years and AMARC became home for many of these prototype airframes such as the Fairchild T-46 trainer, the Piper Enforcer close air support fighter and both the YC-14 and YC-15 STOL transport. Many NASA test aircraft are also stored here.

Various fire bomber programs have used AMARC aircraft such as the S-2, C-47, C-118, C-119, P2V and C-130. Davis-Monthan is also well represented in the cargo fleets of many smaller air forces by C-7s, C-46s, C-47s, C-54s, C-97s, C-118s, C-121s, and C-131s.

The taxpayer has benefited by transfers of surplus military aircraft to other government agencies such as police departments, forestry agencies, U.S. Customs, Civil Defense, the Civil Air Patrol, Department of Agriculture, and numerous vo-tech schools. The sales of surplus T-28 Trojans for the warbird community has been particularly brisk.

Most of the aircraft that reach civilian markets get there via dealers who bid on the aircraft up for sale. Usually, the aircraft are sold on a lot basis rather than one by one. A large percentage of these aircraft are towed to one of the many gates leading off base where they are transferred to the buyer who tows them to his nearby yard. After rework and FAA checks, the planes are towed back to the base and flown out. Reportedly, there is a requirement for $1 million in insurance to fly off the runway at Davis-Monthan.

Thousands of surplus aircraft have gone to friendly foreign countries such as S-2 Trackers to Korea, Taiwan, Peru, Venezuela, Australia and Uruguay; T-33 Shooting Stars to Mexico, Taiwan and Columbia; A-4 Skyhawks to Singapore and Malaysia; and F-4J Phantoms to the Royal Air Force.

The Mexican Armed Forces have recently purchased a number of surplus T-33s and had them refurbished. The refurbishment work included zero-timing the engine, airframe supports, avionics updates and hardpoints for bombs or rockets. An attractive package for an air force on a limited budget.

At a casual glance the AMARC yard looks rather sedate. But it is actually a beehive of activity, constantly in transition.

There are no less than sixty Boeing B-52 bombers parked in this area of AMARC. A sight like this is reminiscent of post-World War II when D-M was filled with B-17s, B-24s and B-29s. (Fugere/AMARC)

A number of late model Lockheed P2V Neptunes have been converted as fire bombers on the civil market. This is an SP-2H with underwing jet engines and wing tip fuel tanks. (Wonderly)

An overall Natural Metal Douglas C-47D formerly of the South Vietnamese Air Force. The Vietnamese were the recipients of a large number of aircraft removed from the facility during the war years. (Kula)

This A-7E (BuNo 157466) carries the tail code NJ, identifying it as being assigned to VA-122 Flying Eagles. VA-122 was the light attack readiness squadron providing A-7 transition training for West coast units. (Dunham)

This Marine Corps Phantom was flown in by VMFA-235 Death Angels. The F-4S was a former F-4J (Buno 158373) rebuilt to F-4S standards. (Dunham)

This T-28B Trojan, formerly assigned to VT-27, NAS Corpus Christi, Texas, will most probably find a new home in the hands of a warbird enthusiast. Her radial engine is preserved in the boxed engine canister in front of the aircraft. (Wonderly)

This Republic F-84F Thunderstreak is in the process of being restored for donation to a museum. The aircraft was being put together from several different F-84F airframes. (Wonderly)

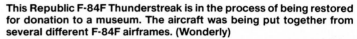

A McDonnell-Douglas A-4L Skyhawk from VC-2 displays its special bicenntenial color scheme. This aircraft has since departed for Malaysia where it served as a source of spare parts for the fleet of A-4PTMs flown by the Malaysian Air Force. (Puzzullo)

Sitting on the far end of the transient ramp, this C-121 was in the final stages of preparation for the flight to Charleston, S.C. Although a little tarnished around the edges, the Connie was in good condition. The aircraft now carries the civilian registration N88879. (Wonderly)

Most of the aircraft parts reclamation work takes place in the open storage yard at AMARC. The wings are already removed and the vertical stabilizer is being removed from this Lockheed VC-141 Jetstar. (Wonderly)

The aircraft stored at AMARC, such as this Convair T-29, provide an unbelievable amount of surplus parts that are either reused, sold, or broken up and melted down. (Wonderly)

Many aircraft, such as this C-118, have too many flight hours on their airframes to meet civil certification and are placed in special parts reclaiming areas. Here they are stripped of usable parts. (Wonderly)

This stripped Air Force Systems Command NC-135A was an early model aircraft used as a testbed. The parts salvaged from this aircraft are used on active duty KC-135s still in the USAF inventory. (Wonderly)

Many of the older aircraft in long term storage at D-M are being held for military and civilian museums. This EC-121 is one of the few that still exists; most Connies have been sold off or scrapped. (Wonderly)

This LTV A-7A Corsair II formerly attached to VA-304 is now flying for the Portugese Air Force. A number of PAF A-7Ps started out as ex-U.S. Navy A-7As and A-7Bs from AMARC. (Puzzullo)

The Douglas F3D/F-10 Skynight was still operating during the 1960s with the Marine Corps as the EF-10 and with the U.S. Army as a platform for testing air-to-air missiles. This ex-Navy aircraft is one of only five left at AMARC. (Wonderly)

Two Lockheed T-33 Shooting Stars await a ferry flight to a rework facility. South and Central American Air Forces have done well with reconditioned T-Birds, some of which are armed and serve a dual role as trainers and ground support aircraft. (Kula)

This Grumman E-2B Hawkeye lacks a nosewheel and requires the support of stands as the slow process of parts reclamation takes its toll on the airframe. There are only a few E-2A/B Hawkeyes currently stored at AMARC. (Wonderly)

This ex-Navy F-10 Douglas Skynight is one of five left at AMARC. The aircraft has been stripped of a number of its major components, as well as the wheels off the main landing gear struts. (Wonderly)

The F-104D Starfighter was a two seat operational trainer variant of the F-104C Starfighter for Tactical Air Command. After some fifteen years of storage this Starfighter is missing its landing gear, canopies and nose radome. (Wonderly)

A P-3A Orion formerly of VP-92 at NAS South Weymouth, rests on wooden stands after having relinquished her landing gear and other major parts to keep other P-3s in a flyable condition. (Wonderly)

Virtually any special pallet or loading package can be custom built at AMARC. This USAF T-39 Sabreliner sits on a platform, minus its wings, ready to be loaded on a flatbed for transport to its next destination. (Wonderly)

This immaculately maintained Douglas VC-118B was formerly assigned to Headquarters, U.S. Marine Corps at Quantico, Virginia. Shortly after its arrival in 1983, it was sold to a civil operator. (Puzzullo)

One of the two Piper PA-48 Enforcer prototypes in storage at AMARC was donated to a museum. It was neatly crated up for shipment to the museum with Spraylat still protecting the aircraft. (Wonderly)

During February of 1989, VC-118 427, still carrying her Marine Corps markings, was at Tucson International Airport being returned to service as a civil freighter. (Dunham)

Last Flight

Those aircraft that do not go on to a new life as fire bombers, foreign frontline equipment, or to civilian owners, are destined to one of several fates. Generally, these aircraft either go to a museum or, after being stripped of usable parts, are consigned to the smelter.

There is a large salvage industry around the edges of Davis-Monthan. Several dealers in the scrap metal business are also in the aircraft parts business, while others are in the aircraft resale business.

When an aircraft is purchased, if it is not airworthy or cannot be made airworthy, it is usually used as a source of spare parts. All usable parts are taken off the aircraft including everything from wheel sets to seats. Scrap items must be separated with the aluminum sorted out from other metals, rubber or plastics.

Once this is completed the airframe is cut into smaller sections by torch, dragline type booms, or large steel blades which are dropped by a crane. Gas charged furnaces reduce the aluminum into ingots that are then shipped to recycling centers. These ingots are used to produce cans, aluminum siding, pots and pans, and other aluminum products.

Some aircraft, however, are kept and stripped of parts as needed. Combat type aircraft are made unflyable by cutting through the wing and tailplane roots so they cannot be sold to unfriendly parties.

Some aircraft are retired to duty as a gate guard or as part of a museum. Many aircraft within the facility gates are being stored for museums until they have space or can arrange for transport. A classic example was the prototype Boeing B-707 "Dash 80" prototype owned by the Smithsonian. The aircraft was stored until the Summer of 1991 when it was flown out to Boeing for restoration prior to being put on display. Throughout the years a major portion of the U.S. military aircraft on display in museums have come from AMARC.

One of the prime aviation museums is the Pima Air Museum in Tucson, Arizona. Founded during 1966 and covering some thirty acres, this museum houses a large collection of aircraft. Pima's proximity to Davis-Monthan gives it a great advantage in obtaining aircraft for display.

All of the aircraft at AMARC, the Pima Air Museum, the Tucson Airport and in the civilian yards serve as silent reminders of our aviation heritage. They are all Ladies - in - Waiting. Waiting for their ultimate fate — good or bad. In many ways, this facility is providing not only an ending for the aircraft, but for many a new beginning.

A row of six ex-Navy UH-1 Huey trainer helicopters parked at a resale yard. Most aircraft are sold to the civilian market in lots at public auctions. (Wonderly)

These C-130A Hercules transports are parked in a yard off base among old engines and parts. The U.S. Forestry Department recently acquired a number of surplus C-130s for conversion to fire bombers. (Wonderly)

This Navy Lockheed T-33B from Naval Air Station Key West, Florida has been in storage since the mid-1960s. She has been promised to a museum. (Wonderly)

A dozen C-47 Skytrains sit patiently waiting to give up parts or become rebuilt aircraft. This civilian storage yard specializes in rebuilding C-47s for the civil market. (Wonderly)

Two QF-100 Super Sabre drones on the ramp at Mojave. These aircraft are entering the third and last phase of their service lives, after distinguished service as frontline and later ANG fighter bombers. (Puzzullo)

The T-28 Trojan was the last radial engined training aircraft to be used by the U.S. military. This ex-Marine T-28B was formerly based at Marine Corps Headquarters, Quantico, Virginia. The aircraft was sold and will probably end up on the warbird circuit. (Wonderly)

A short walk through the yard of a surplus aircraft parts dealer will give you a new appreciation of just how many individual parts make up an aircraft. (Wonderly)

This ex-Navy C-131F (BuNo 141026) was formerly attached to NAS Bermuda. About 825 nautical miles due East of Savannah, NAS Bermuda is a converted Air Force Base. It is now an important base for anti-submarine operations and serves as home to a number of rotating P-3 Orions. (Wonderly)

These rows of ex-United States Navy Piasecki (later Vertol) H-25 Retriever helicopters have been in open storage for many years in a salvage yard off base. (Wonderly)

A Curtiss C-46 Commando awaits a new owner in a civilian yard off base. This aircraft is in a poor state of repair, but, hopefully, it may become part of a museum. The insignia on the tail is a winged Tiger emblem. (Wonderly)

A Grumman F-11 Tiger in the markings of the Naval Air Test Center sits on the desert floor minus its wings and tail surfaces. This aircraft had been used in an experimental in-flight thrust control program. (Wonderly)

This surplus Douglas C-117 "Super Goonie" has been reworked and polished by a civil aircraft dealer for a second career hauling freight for a small civil air cargo line. (Wonderly)

During 1972, Boeing and McDonnell-Douglas were awarded contracts to build prototypes of an advanced medium STOL transport to replace the C-130 Hercules. The Boeing YC-14 prototype featured two GE turbofan engines in overwing pods. (Wonderly)

Hayes aircraft converted eighty-two of these ex-ANG Boeing KC-97L tankers to the "Ultimate KC-97" standard with two J-47-GE-25A jet pods on underwing pylons instead of the usual auxiliary fuel tanks. (Wonderly).

The end of the road for many aircraft is the guillotine, torch and furnace. All of this work is done off base. Some of the major breaking up of aircraft has been done in the past on the base, but this has now stopped. (Wonderly)

The McDonnell-Douglas YC-15 entry featured four Pratt & Whitney turbofan engines (removed). Budget problems cancelled the program after four aircraft were completed. (Wonderly)

The only known combat aircraft outside the AMARC fence are these A-4 Skyhawks. Under the Military Assistance Program (MAP) contract, only a certain number per year may leave this compound for rework in Singapore to the A-4S and A-4S-1 standard. (Wonderly)

Fortunately there is still a market for radial engined aircraft. This HU-16 Albatross has been sold to one of the local dealers near the base. During 1988 it was undergoing restoration for delivery to its civil owner. (Wonderly)

An endless variety of aircraft in all sizes can be seen at Tucson International. This Lockheed C-82 Packet transport was parked at the Tucson airport along with a C-45 and a B-26 Invader. (Wonderly)

The North American F-107A lost the production contract to the Republic F-105 and only three were ever built. The Pima Air Museum's F-107A was the first one built. One crashed and the other is at the U.S. Air Force Museum in Dayton, Ohio. (Wonderly)

The quality of the restoration work at Pima is evident in the pristine condition of this North American F-86H Sabre. In all, some 9,502 Sabres were built and the aircraft was used by twenty-one countries. (Dunham)

This Navy Grumman F6F-3 Hellcat sat on the ocean floor for thirty years. It was ditched off San Diego during 1944 after the engine failed and was raised during 1974. The pilot who survived the incident has visited the aircraft at Pima. (Wonderly)

The Boeing 307 Stratoliner was a passenger transport version of the famous B-17. It was also the first passenger airliner with a pressurized cabin. This aircraft was last used by Papa Doc Duvalier and was part of the Haitian Air Force. It is on loan to Pima by the National Air and Space Museum. (Wonderly)

This ex-TWA Lockheed C-69 Constellation was the tenth airframe built. It flew for the AAF from 1945-48, then was sold to TWA. The aircraft has 41,908 hours total flying time. The beautiful restoration was carried out by a TWA crew on their own time at Pima. (Dunham)

The Pima Air Museum's Consolidated B-24J Liberator was donated to the Museum by the Government of India. It was flown to Arizona during 1969, taking thirty-one days to complete the trip from India. (Wonderly)

A SAC Convair B-58A Hustler. The B-58 set more world records than any other combat aircraft in USAF history. Pima's B-58 was the last one built. (Wonderly)

Pima's Martin PBM-5A Mariner served in both World War II and Korea. There were some 1,235 PBM flying boats built and this is the only known Mariner remaining. (Wonderly)

This P2V-7 Neptune at Pima was remanufactured as an AP-2H during 1967 for service in Vietnam. This aircraft was used extensively in Vietnam and was even damaged by small arms fire during 1968. (Dunham)